SOARING SOULS:

THE DAWNING OF A NEW ERA

EILEEN CURTEIS

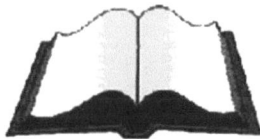

CCB Publishing
British Columbia, Canada

Soaring Souls: The Dawning of a New Era

Copyright ©2009 by Eileen Curteis
ISBN-13   978-1-926585-59-8
First Edition

Library and Archives Canada Cataloguing in Publication

Curteis, Eileen, 1942-
Soaring souls : the dawning of a new era /
written and illustrated by Eileen Curteis.
ISBN 978-1-926585-59-8
I. Title.
PS8555.U84S59 2009   C813'.54   C2009-905989-4

Cover art and interior pastel drawings by Eileen Curteis.

Publisher: CCB Publishing
             British Columbia, Canada
             www.ccbpublishing.com

To become a lighthouse

for God…

these are the friends

I walk with

INTRODUCTION

THE NEW FACE OF GOD

If there is a rumour out there that God is dead, this book will shatter the old image of a God in the sky who punishes us for being bad. And if there is such a thing as naughty children locking themselves in a closet for fear of being found, it will not be God that shuts the door on them.

In this third millennium, perhaps we're all coming of age and seeing for ourselves that it's happening now – the Love we've all been hungering for. Whether we see it or not, it's on our doorsteps, this new face of God with wide open wings soaring toward us. Even if we try we cannot stop its momentum. Some perhaps will fear it and go back into their sheltered homes. Others will welcome it like cyclists finding their first wind.

Soaring Souls: The Dawning of a New Era, is about this awakening, this hunger to know God more. Originally, this book began as a short story written in the winter of 1975 when a married woman momentarily left her home to find the God she was seeking. Her mystical story and that of her soul-soaring friend is based on the metaphor of a tree, somewhat gnarled and disfigured, until Divine Love invades the branches of both of them.

Today, thirty-four years later, this same story has been pulled down off the shelf, dusted off, taken out of the cupboard and is ready now for a second viewing. Obviously, the honeymoon is over. Reality has set in and, yet, the call of the true mystic knows that you don't fall in love with God once but you do it over and over again. How you do it doesn't matter. You just do it.

One day you're a cocoon, stumbling out of the old skin into the new one; then it's a butterfly, a wasp, a bee. There's no end to your becoming. It's an ethereal ride on a mundane motor scooter, an earthly jog, which never quite reaches its destination.

This book reminds us that we are all spiritual adventurers on the move, sometimes basking in the sun, sometimes falling into the land called too barren to live in. Whenever or wherever Love finds us, she does not squeeze the breath out of us. She is the pivotal mother standing on the edge of our tragedy, teaching us to walk in it with soft shoes comfortable enough to have a padding in them. More than anyone, she rejoices in the beauty of our ripening before we do.

Whenever we lean into Love in this way, even a whisper of it, the ears of our souls will perk up their antennae and say to this evolutionary God – we have known you, seen you, touched you, loved you. You are the reason we are here, the fountain spilling over in us. If you keep pursuing us, we will not hide ourselves from you nor will we sit idle in a corner. Instead, we will open our wings to the rush and flow of your Energy.

As much as we would like to stay in these ethereal zones, Love reminds us that the plunge back into the real world of the here and now is often where the greatest learning takes place. If we come to know that each of us is the mouth-piece of God we may be surprised to find that the encyclopaedia of life can be learned from one another. So why not knock on the door of our neighbour to find that the heart of God lives there?

And what about the changing of the seasons? Do we open our weary souls to this kind of restoration and if we do where does God fit into the framework of our minds? Do we take this author of life for granted or is there perhaps a bit of the scientist in us saying, "Prove your existence." In the downtimes of life if we could just let that first song of a bird in spring send us into ecstasy we wouldn't be asking for a definition of God. We would just accept Divine mystery as it is and let God be God.

If this book has anything to tell us it will be this - God is never tedious about our becoming. Even if we lose our way and become lethargic on the journey, God will find us in our most deserted places, and like children on a seesaw going up and down we will come to know the beauty of our rising and falling. There will never be a time when Love doesn't welcome us. Even when our tongues run dry and words fail us, Love will be there with her Divine compass to guide us toward the land we long for.

DEDICATION

Katreyn, this is your story and you are the inspiration behind it. I have written it for you and for all the people who are like you – beautiful in the way they live and in the Song they sing.

It is my way of saying thank you for being who you are. It makes the journey so much easier finding a friend like you to soar with.

I want you to know that I am grateful to you for laying down your life in the most noble way that you can and for following those aspirations which are highest to you.

It is my belief that you have been specially chosen to follow a spiritual quest which will cause you to run in the direction of the Beloved for the remainder of your days.

I hope that as you read these pages you will come to understand a little better the destiny of us yellowbirds, who fly not according to the norms of others but according to some great Spirit who enters into our lives at the precise moment when we are ready.

Written in the winter months of 1975.

JOURNEY OF A MYSTIC

Katreyn Baylon, age twenty-nine, left the home of her husband, Cremin, on the night of Tuesday, October 24th at 7:00 pm. She had left home many times before, but tonight for some unknown reason there was something different about her going. Her eldest son, Kristof, turned out the lights after her as if he knew she had to make some kind of journey alone. Nicolene, although she was only two, kissed her mother with more fervour than usual and Stefan and Erin just waved. Cremin's smile had been slow in coming as if he, too, knew but when it did come it explained everything about who he was and why Katreyn had chosen him in the first place. Perhaps better than anyone she had understood and penetrated those dark eyes which held within them the unspeakable depth and tenderness of his love for her. Knowing all this and the bliss which human love had provided her, there was still something wanting in the heart of Katreyn, Something which even she could not penetrate, Something which was slowly drawing her out of herself in a search which was more than earthbound. Why she had to go only she knew and if anyone were to suffer it would not be her family whom she had loved passionately but herself

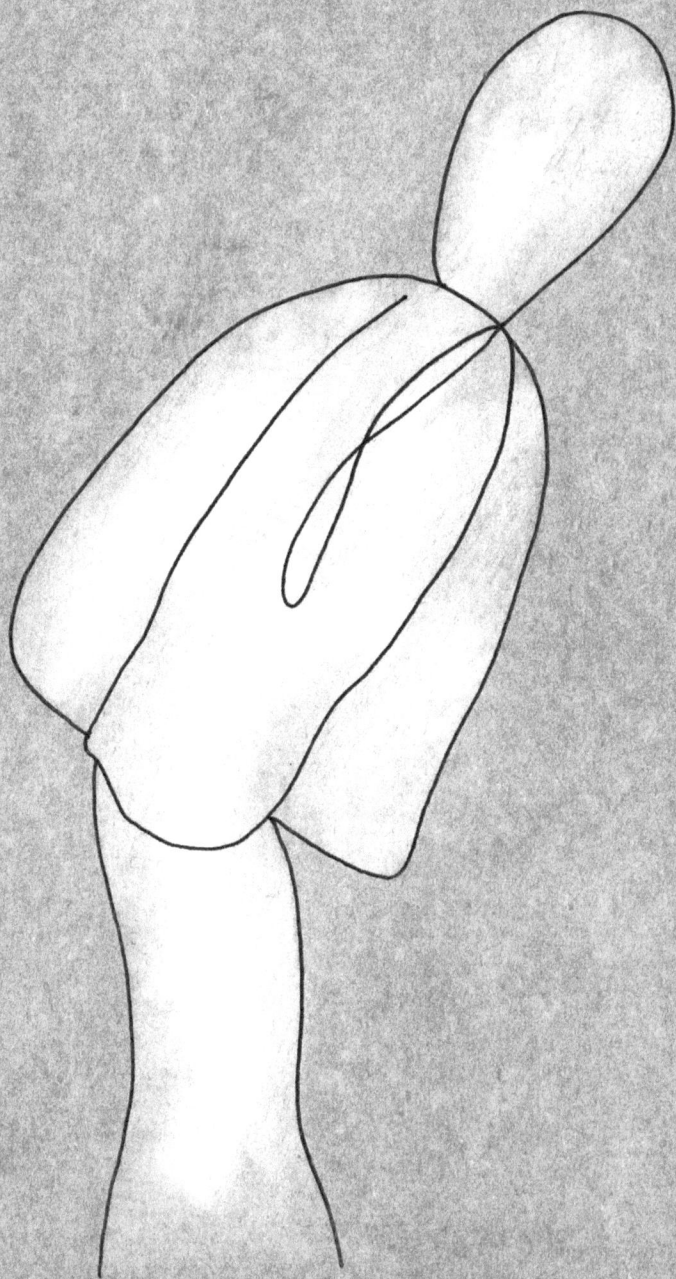

DARK NIGHT

whom she had never loved enough.

Softly she said: "I'll be back Cremin. Don't wait up for me." Quietly she closed the door behind her. The lights which Kristof had turned out made it seem darker than ever as slowly she made her way up the hill to the place of her second commitment. She had only made two commitments in her life – the first to Cremin and the second to Someone greater than Cremin.

She was alone now in the crisp, cool air of night. There were no stars to greet her this time, just a deliberate moon and a darker than usual sky that was slowly pressing its fingers around her like a stranger in the night, a stranger that wanted to squeeze from her some kind of a death of a different order. What was the meaning of this Hand, she asked herself? And why did she – Katreyn Baylon – have to be caught in the clutches of it?

Deafened by her own footsteps, she made her way up to the highway, reassuring herself that surely someone in one of the cars would provide her with the explanation she was looking for but no one provided her with anything. They just whizzed by her slender, beautiful form as though

KATREYN'S ALONE JOURNEY

she were a part of the pavement that people travel on but never fully appreciate.

Crossing the street on her own, she knew now not to expect anything from anyone. No one would help her and she was sure of that.

Stopping at the first tree she came to, she flung her body against the hardest part of its trunk. Then rising with what strength she had left in her, she grappled with its branches until she could grapple no more. Letting go, she slid beneath the ground into the roots of where her own passions lay. Only poets do this. And she – Katreyn Baylon – had always been a poet. Right from the moment of conception in her mother's womb, she had always been a poet.

Wet with tears, she waited for an answer that the tree could not give her. What was she to do? And where was she to go? And would he – Cremin Baylon – ever understand that though she loved him more than any other single human being on this earth there was One who had taken

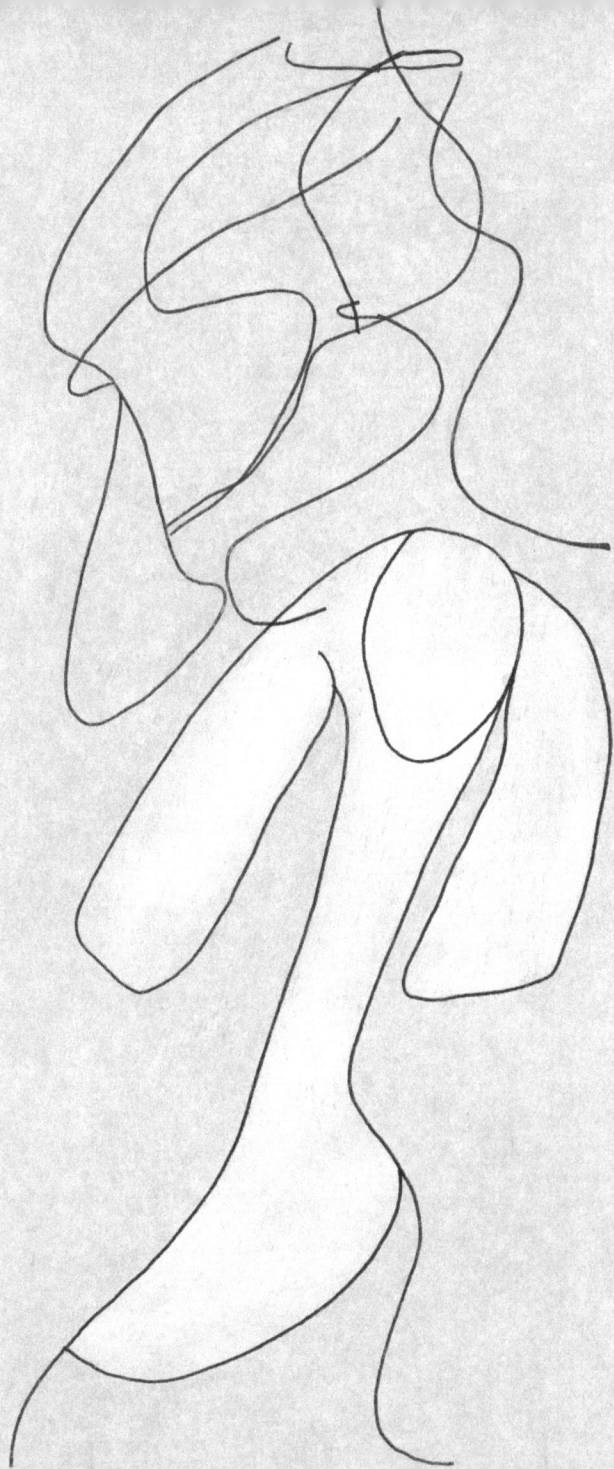

TREE STRUGGLE

precedence over him? And what about her family? How could they possibly understand? Passionately she would love them, she told herself, not less but more. But would they understand her walking from now on? She had no assurance that they would.

As she raised her eyes, she saw that the house on the hill was waiting for her. She would go into it as she had gone into her own home. But would her Beloved be there she asked herself? Or was it just some kind of foolish emotion that had set her feet to travelling in this new way?

Others were in the room when she got there – sitting in armchairs or on couches – talking more than listening.

Slowly she sat down in the chair at the farthest corner of the room. That was a good place for her she told herself. She always had been different and if anything were to happen to her tonight it would be better that she were away from the crowd than in the midst of them.

Did they really know her she asked herself? Or would it be like all those other groups she had

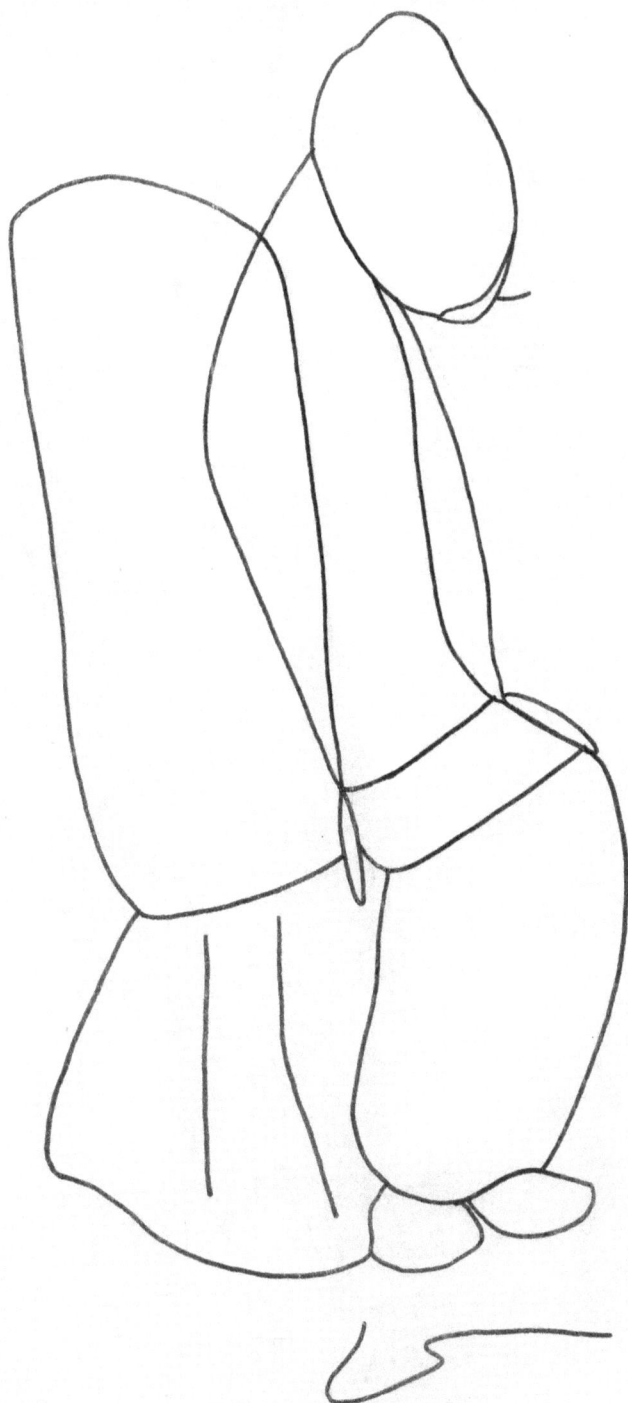

CORNER CHAIR

been in, where what you are is pushed into the background of your subconscious mind. Would they, she wondered, be any different or would they, too, force her to wear some false kind of a cover-up when what she really wanted to wear was the face that was her own.

And would there be anybody in the group who would recognize her desires as part of their own and if there was would they be so good as to listen to her who needed more than the roots of a tree to absorb her in the days that lay ahead.

It was just as she was forming these thoughts into a prayer that she saw and recognized the face that was not unlike her own. There in the group, sitting just as quietly as herself, she saw in the eyes of the person across from her the friend who held within her gaze the answer as to why she had come this night and not some other night.

And then it happened, what Katreyn had hoped would happen – two spirits unlocking themselves from the inside, flinging the doors of their cages wide open so as to leave the room in which they were physically present for that of a more permanent dwelling. Flying at terrifically

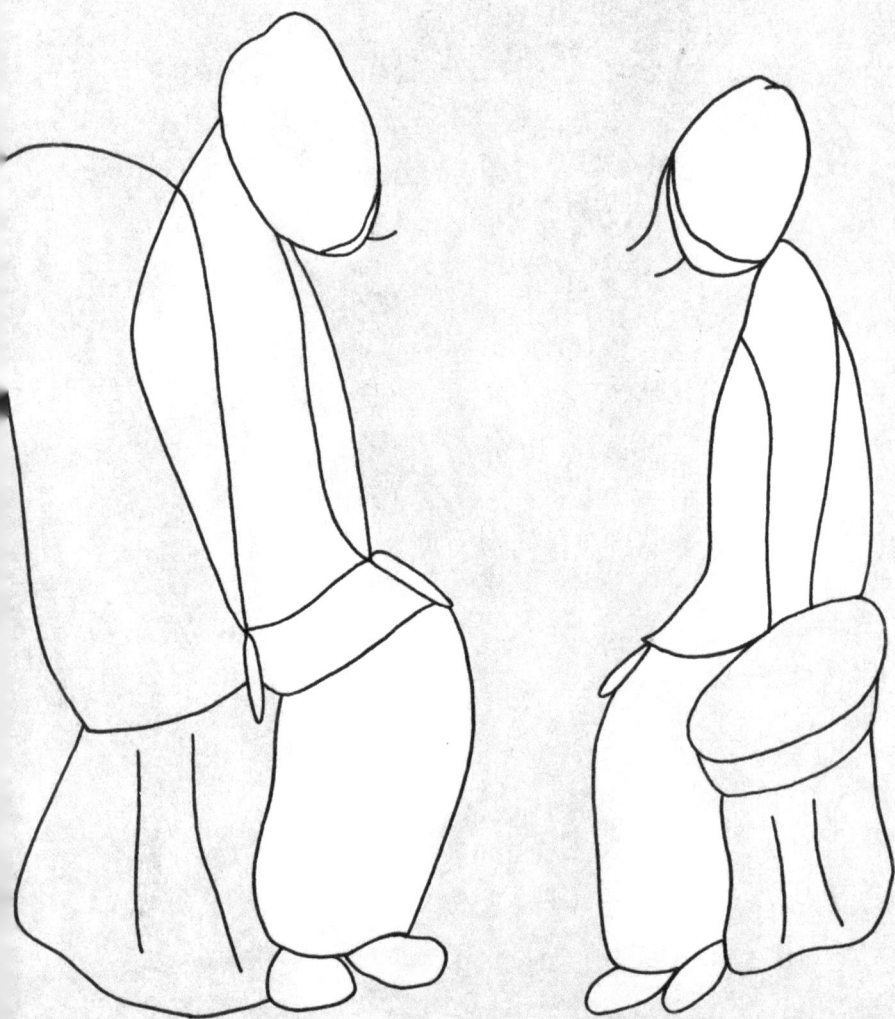

THE LISTENERS

great speeds they left the universe of humankind to find in one another the release of their aspirations that had been born for this hour. Of course, this all sounds ridiculous to someone who has not had such an experience and to try and explain it to someone who has never journeyed beyond the bars of their own cage would be, you understand, an impossible task.

The crowd was far behind now, unconscious and unaware that our spiritual souls had even left the room. As for ourselves, we had sold everything human that would weigh us down so as to enter into the realms of a further climb.

Together, we did things we had never done before. She, Katreyn, soared along the horizon of her being. And I, Kayleen, commended her for her efforts. Nothing was too much for us. Every peak was the mountain of a further summit.

As we neared the heights, Katreyn turned to me waiting for some kind of a response. Little did she realize that I had been waiting all of eleven years to find a bird of her description who

SPIRIT SOULS

would fly beyond the limits of our physical universe.

Turning to her in the breeze, I placed my wing in hers, as the seal of our spiritual marriage together. And then I spoke in a way which had never been given me to speak, knowing that she who stood beside me had been afforded the same unspeakable vision of the Kingdom which is given to anyone who has enough keenness of soul to search it out. And so…I began my song to one whose Beauty lay in her power to listen.

Flying beside her, I told her that there were no bars in the Kingdom, just beautiful open windows and doors where sun-born people live and that what you looked like or what you were didn't matter here.

Turning to me, she seemed to understand everything without my explaining anything. And then she greeted me with the silent gaze of why she had come. And I who had known all along, recognized her as the one I had been looking for, the one that had for so long now been hidden in

SUMMIT WALKERS

my poet's dream, and so I told her who she was…

A yellowbird with golden wings

flying high

with the voice

of a song bird…

A winged wanderer

whose only home lay

in the Source of her vision.

No sooner had I spoken to Katreyn in this way, than I knew it was time for me to leave. It was hard saying good-bye. And, yet, this is one of the rules of the Kingdom. You can't hold on to anyone, unless you choose to. And then, of course, the journey ends.

I told her that this was only the beginning of our meetings and that much of what I wanted to tell her she would have to learn on her own. We hadn't really had a chance to talk about suffering but something inside of me told me that she

WINGED WANDERERS

understood it well and that when we would meet again she would understand it even better.

"Good-bye" I said. "This is the door by which you came in. It leads back to the home of your responsibility. Go gently now, into the night. Remember what you have learned and apply it well."

"Thank you" she said. "Thank you. I will do just as you say, for never would it have happened had I not come."

Everything was different now. The lights had been left on behind her and the whole sky knew about her vision, that she – Katreyn Baylon – would not harm a single soul in sight, for deep within her burned a Love that had etched its face of radiance on every tree that stood before her.

Running down the hill, no one had to tell her who she was. She just knew it by the song that every creature sang and felt it deep within her the Song of her own wanderings.

KATREYN'S DEPARTURE

Like a mystic in the night, she had become for a moment what this world never lets you become – a soaring bird, an uncluttered spirit, a song writer who was beginning to compose her own lyrics.

After travelling this way for the few short hours that she had, she stopped to catch her breath, disheartened by the downward flight of a bird which lay heavy on her.

"Oh bird!" she cried.

"What is the meaning of this downward motion? Are you, too, like the others, come to deceive me when I had set you up as my journey's end?"

But the bird, pretending not to hear her, flew away with not so much as turning its head.

Silenced by the darkness of night and calmed by her own inwardness, she returned to her former state, only to find herself standing beneath the branches of a tree that had no more seen her

SOUL SONG

bird than she had.

Somewhat saddened by her return, she let the wind enter her with its own twinges of loneliness. Then raising her eyes, as if to speak, she felt the cool sap from the tree running through her body like a stream in the night.

Overcome by happiness, she fell to the ground weeping as she had never wept before and heaven wept with her as she – Katreyn Baylon – gave birth to a better way.

Lifting her head, she saw her name on every living thing, a name which was above all other names for its humility and for the way in which it had travelled.

Stretching forth her arms to the furthest parts of the universe, she saw for the first time who she was and embraced herself as the woman of integrity who had stepped outside of her home a few hours previous in search of a destiny that would slowly be revealed.

Standing inside her vision, she beheld how far she had come and how far she had yet to go and with what kind of a soaring she would have to move if the attainment of her second commitment

DOWNWARD FLIGHT

were to be as much a part of her as Cremin's coming had been the first time.

Leaning against her favourite tree, she knew the time had come, for like the tree she too was ripe for some kind of a picking. What the nature of it was she couldn't exactly say, or what would be its demands she didn't know that either. But what she did know was that she – Katreyn Baylon, poet of the universe – for having travelled a different road on a different night would be from now on a stranger to a world that was incapable of understanding the dimensions to which the Beloved was calling her.

"Oh, tree," she whispered.

"Now that you have brought me this far, does it mean that from now on there will be no one?"

"Not exactly," said the tree.

"But there will be fewer, just because of the direction in which you are moving."

"Oh!" said Katreyn.

"Tell me more, for never as long as I have known myself to be in existence, have I been so

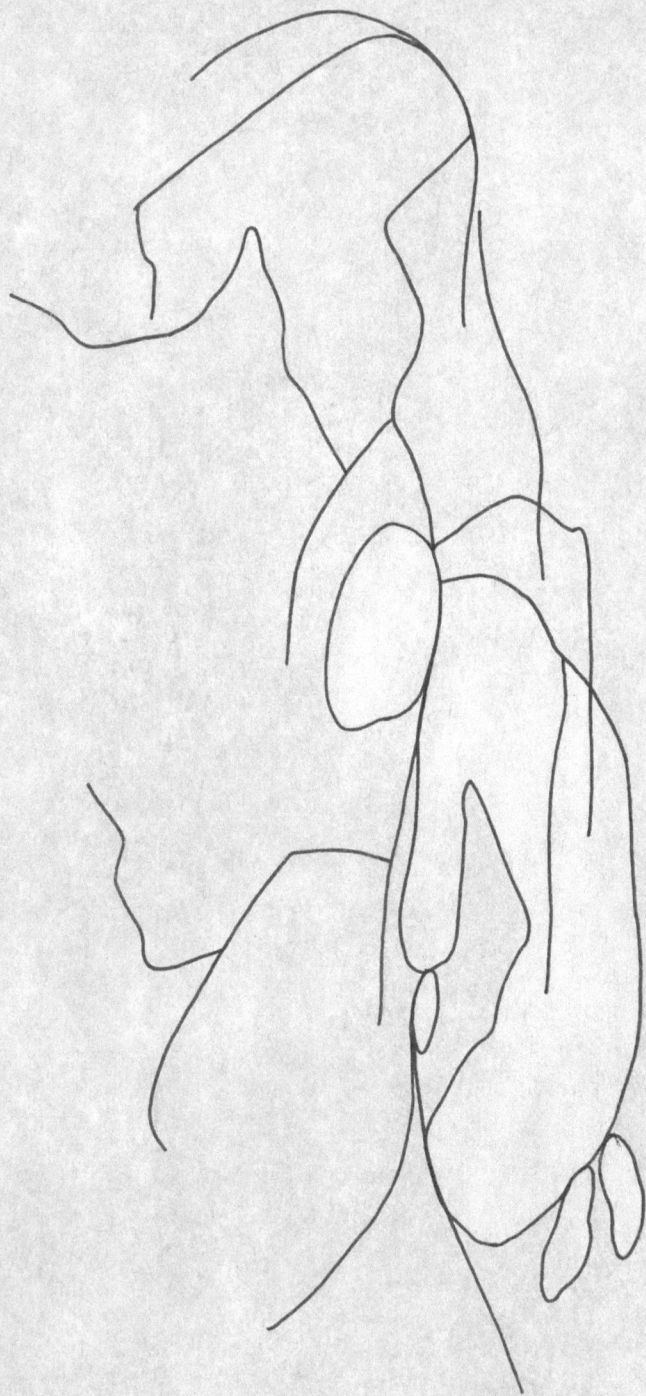

PICKING TIME

committed to following a way such as the one that you are laying down before me."

"That is where you are wrong," said the tree.

"I have never laid down a way for anyone. If you have come it is not because of something I have done but rather because of something you have done. Our meeting has been purely coincidental. That is the way with most poets. And you – Katreyn Baylon – are the first among them."

Turning to go, she felt a deep kinship with the tree that had awarded her first place. It was the kind of a kinship that comes from having suffered something together, and though she couldn't say for sure what that suffering was, she went away from the tree knowing that they bore something in common.

Waving her last good-bye, she started her journey homeward, alone she thought, until she felt the branch of a tree grabbing at the button of her coat, as if to say there was something in her that was not as yet unclothed for the winter she had to undergo. What had really happened was that Katreyn had left before the tree had spoken

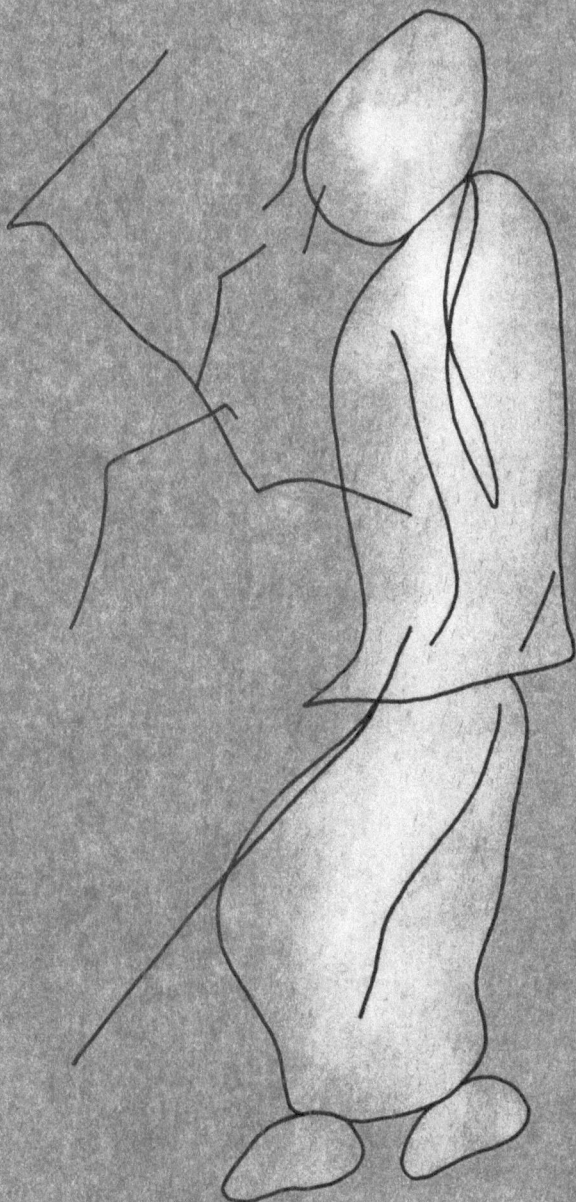

WINTER'S UNCLOTHING

its final word and the action of the branch was the tree's way of getting Katreyn to listen.

Frightened as she was, she threw the branch to one side, believing in both it and the tree and that if either were to speak she would be there to hear.

As a reward for her fidelity, she heard more clearly than she had ever heard before, the voice of her Beloved through the trees.

Oh child of me

the world awaits you to crucify you…

every leaf and flower and bough

for one who stands beside a tree as you do

shall bear a cross in my name

to remind you that you are no greater than I

who hung among these branches before you

for no other reason but that men put me there

to forget about me

even as you shall be forgotten

for having followed.

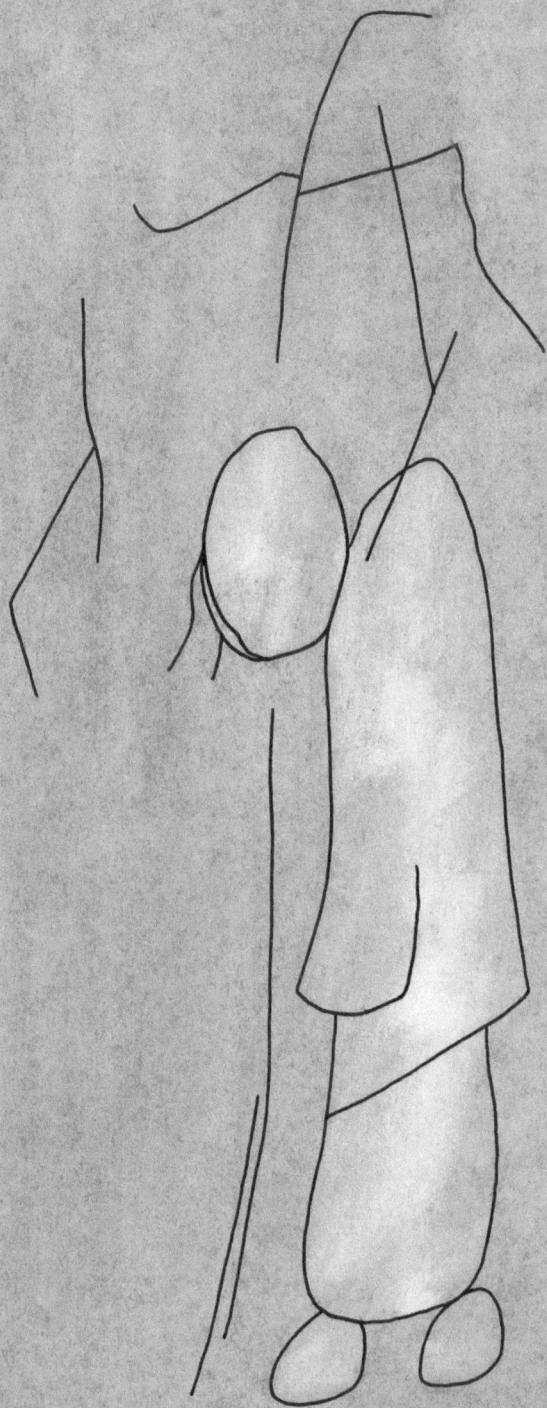

TREE CROSS

Upon hearing these words, Katreyn plunged her twenty-nine year old body into the deepest part of the forest where her Beloved lived. She stood with Him and He with her until they were committed for life.

Never before she told the trees had there been so much greenness in her life and never before had her Beloved come solely for her.

Fingering the trees with utmost care, she felt a ripple of joy run through her. Moments like these are rare, she told herself, and to cling to them would be to deny the gift of the Giver.

Just as she was thinking thoughts like these, her heart gave way and she became a mother again, not that she hadn't always been a mother, but rather she had been elevated for a few short moments to something more than a mother – the mystery of virginity in a woman who longs to bring more to her family than just earthly riches.

It was dark now, as dark as it had been when she first set out – a warning from the elements, perhaps, who saw more clearly than she did the frightful demands to which her destiny was calling her.

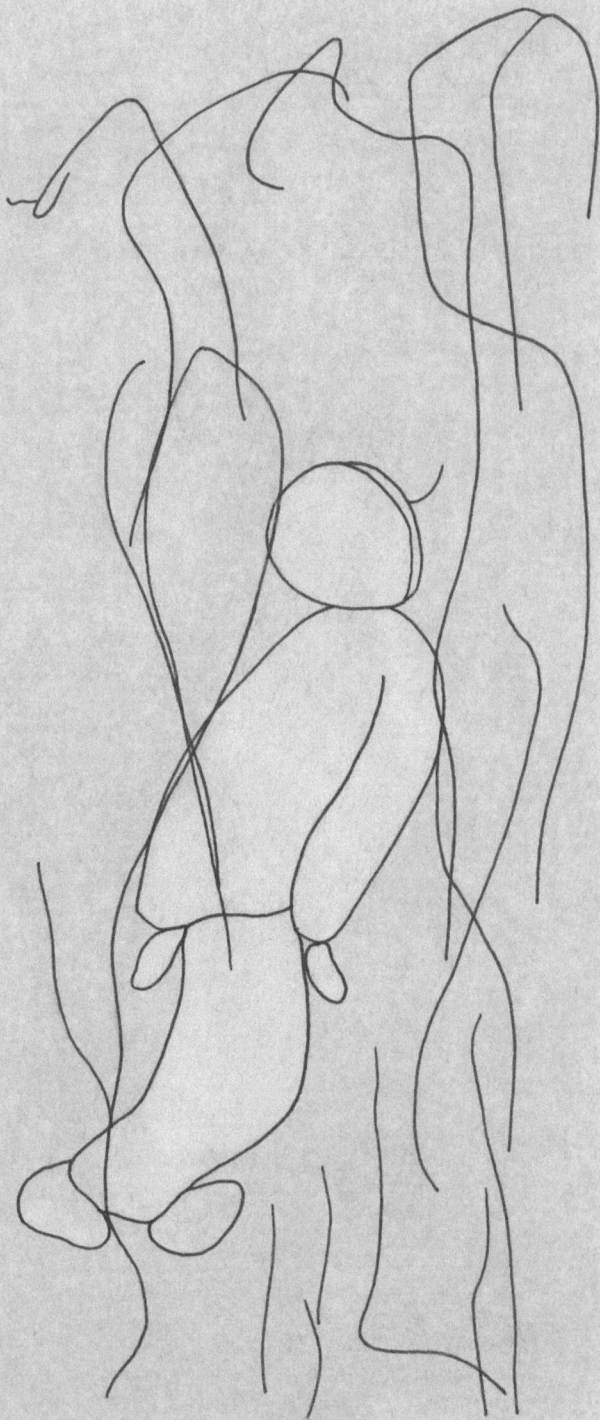

FOREST PLUNGE

Could anyone have comprehended what it was that was being asked of her? I think not. And yet there was something about the deliberateness of the moon which seemed to be shining directly over her, a deliberateness which was lighting up the whole sky.

Was it that she was a messiah? And if she were would they welcome her at the city gates when Him they had turned away? Of course, we have no answers to these questions. But anyone who follows a destiny, as we know Katreyn follows hers, is bound to suffer from the impenetrable walls that people of disbelief have always built and will go on building as long as there is a God and a crucifixion.

But where do we get the strength of a Katreyn, we might ask ourselves, to stand pinned to some kind of a cross as she does? And how do we do it joyfully and in a way which is uncomplaining? How?.....We might well ask ourselves! Because the number is diminishing. And still there is the need to have this story told – the story of how a

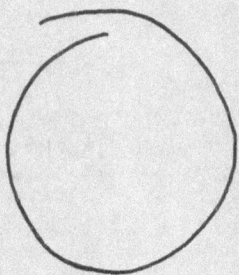

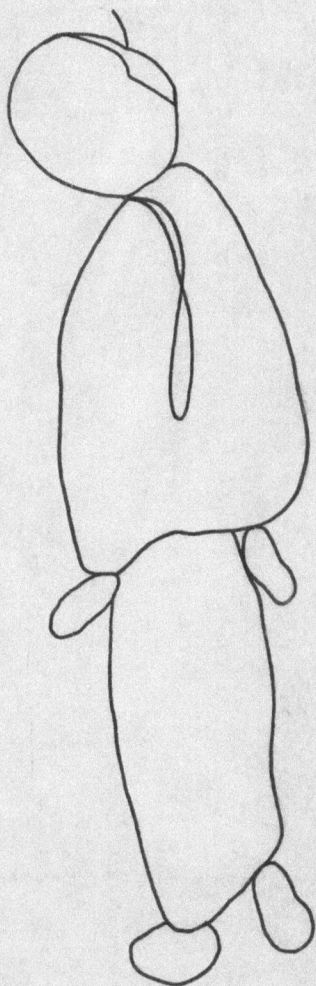

DELIBERATE MOON

Man's Face some two thousand years ago became radiant when he forgave others and of how our faces become radiant, too, when we do it the way he did.

More than anyone else at this time, Katreyn knew that she had grown into a new kind of consciousness. Her walking from now on would be of a different sort and she would know this difference by the pain that it would cause; for what was she but a prophet who had been afforded a vision of Light in a world that so often fails to recognize either the person or the message.

Turning to the trees, she accepted her separateness as a part of what she had come to do, a separateness which would colour her life not only on Francesco Street but wherever she went from now on.

Driven on by the instinct of motherhood, she heard a new voice in the forest. It was Cremin this time, calling her home. It was late now and she could have guessed he would be calling. But why did he have to break into her solitude the

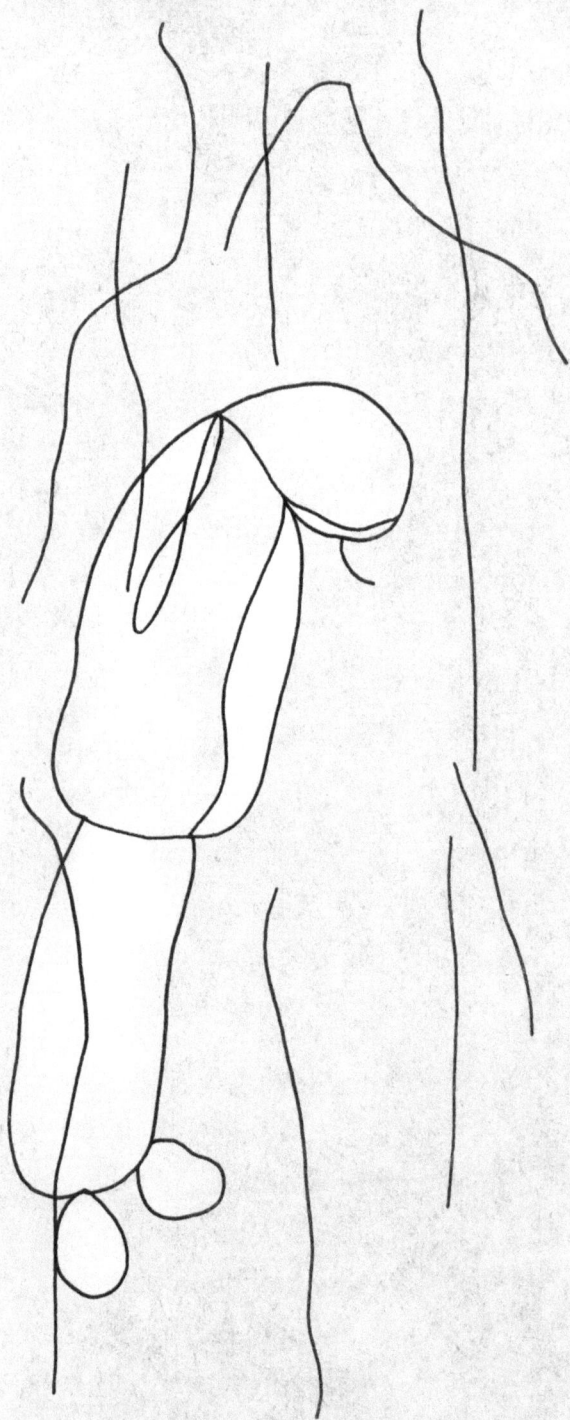

SEPARATE WALKER

way he did? And, Nicolene, why did she have to whimper as though her mother were the only one that could pacify her?

At one time, it would have been easy for Katreyn to have given way to feelings of despondency, but now it was the voice of her Beloved urging her on to a new and better way.

Like a deer in the night, she sped through the forest enkindled by Love. And only Love. No one saw her – not even Cremin. But that was alright she told herself. After all she was a child of the trees and to be forgotten was all part of that kind of a destiny.

Nothing really mattered anymore – just so long as they – Cremin, Nicolene, Erin, Kristof and Stefan would be the recipients of whatever it was that she was meant to bring them.

Seeing Cremin's face for the second time, she clasped it close to hers, wondering if she ever would be able to explain it to him – this marriage of her soul to her Maker. A strange kind of pain gripped her heart as she beheld the face of the man she loved, a face that somehow reminded her of the deepest part of the forest she had been in. And then the answer came to her – a universal

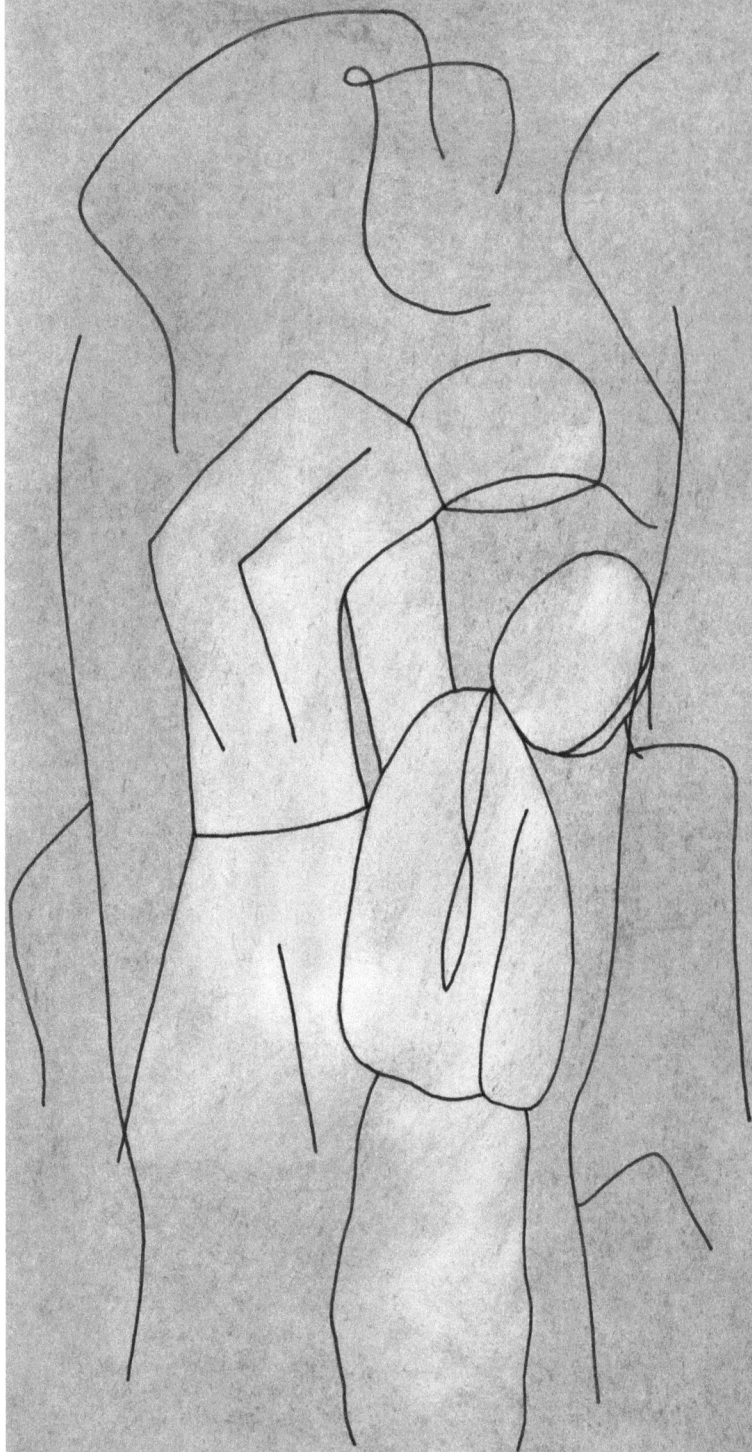

CREMIN'S VOICE

one which needed no explanation – the love of a man for a woman and a woman for her God and how out of that union children have been born for some hour in eternity.

Before leaving the forest for her home on Francesco Street, she felt one last surge of an Infinite and loving presence run through her, a reminder of how she had been chosen and how she must return if the relationship were to further itself. How could she not return she asked herself? For never had anyone shown her the favour that had been hers tonight.

Throwing her hair to one side, she raised her whole being to the One who made her and sang as she had never sung before, a song that was not unlike her Beloved's –

> Dear beautiful One
>
> I have searched for you
>
> all the days of my life
>
> and I have been known
>
> to be slain
>
> by my hunger for you!

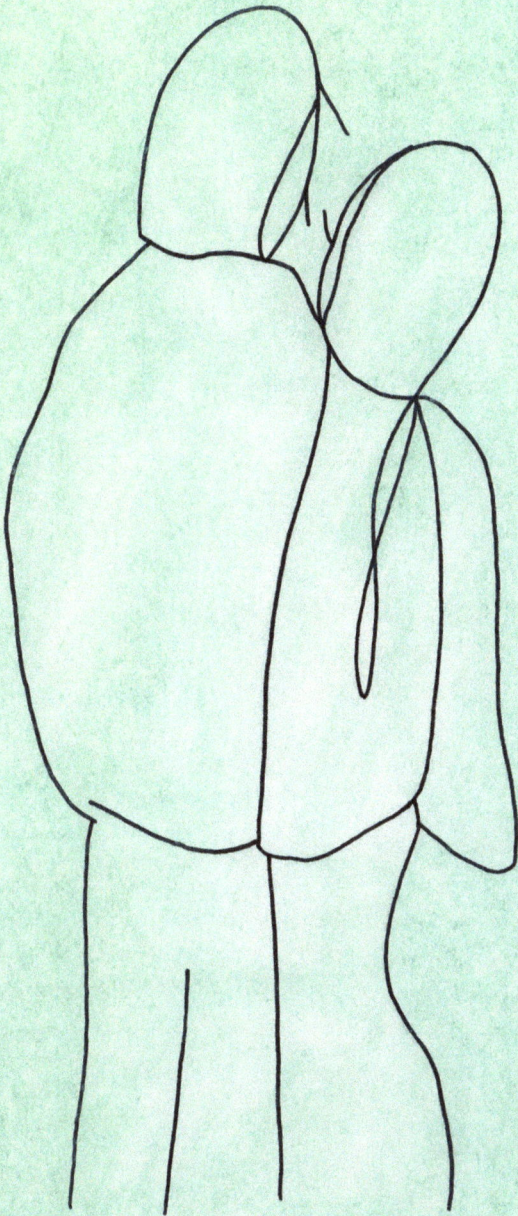

SOUL UNION

Inside your forest, now,

I come

with the bent wing

of a bird

and, oh,

with what gentleness

I lay my feathers

before you.

Carry me, my Beloved,

with the heart

of your splintered footsteps

and when I am gone

from these woods

remember me

to the creatures

I love.

BELOVED FOREST

Her song complete, she left the forest knowing that this would always be home to her and that somehow she would always carry a part of these woods with her wherever she went.

On the pathway, now, which led out to the highway, she paused to catch her breath. It was 12:01, the dawning of a new era, the destined moment of a yellowbird!

NEW ERA

CONCLUSION

THE CALL THAT HAUNTS THE SOUL

It's been thirty-four years now since this story was written. Katreyn has come and gone and in her place there have been so many more Katreyns, each with a story to tell. Men, women, children, people of all ages and nationalities, they keep streaming through the corridor of time. Driven by Love, they seem to be a breed set apart. Highly Spirited and nomadic by nature, you can't put a leash on them. They just go where the Call leads. They are the new Katreyns of the 21st century.

If the Divine rower has set them in motion from the beginning of time, we might ask ourselves – what then makes this generation distinct from those who have gone before? Is it that they paddle their canoes differently or is something more being asked of them? And could it be that the them is us? And if so, are we ready as a human family to become beginners again, to shift gears and go to a school called Divine learning where the traditional way of sitting stationary in our desks is a bygone riveted thing of the past.

As appealing as this third millennium Spirit world may be, not all of us will be ready to jump out of our straight-jackets into a parachute that may appear to be going nowhere, yet obviously Somewhere.

For many of us, it's an exciting era, and even if we try putting the brakes on, this Divine shift will go on creating itself not unlike the force of gravity pushing us forward into a future that is as unpredictable as we are. We might compare it to taking a rowboat out of water and telling it to swim on land. Divine love is like that. It takes you where you never planned to go. You can't force it and, yet, it will bubble up like the ocean when you least expect.

Now for those of us who are Christian, or not; suppose that there was a whirlwind and that the Jesus of history were to return in a rowboat that swept us up into the current of being a lighthouse. Would we be able to stand the brightness of it or would we shrink back into the cradle of our birth?

For the modern day mystics, which is most probably you and I and all of us, it would seem that there is a growing hunger to know God more and that Something is happening! What it is we're not quite sure of but many of us have the uncanny feeling that Something is happening.

Wherever we are on the human journey and whoever we are, it doesn't really matter in the great scheme of things – race, colour, creed, young, old, educational status, rich, poor, healthy, unhealthy, male, female – when it comes to the Love we hanker for, we all need a degree to be expert in it.

Having said this, even if we had the finest book on Love with all the answers in it, the complexity of life for the human journeyer would still remain the same. For faith travellers, though, there are those undoubtedly precious moments when the curtain gets lifted and we see for ourselves, as in a mirror, what it is to be Divinely human. Now suppose that mirror grew into a mammoth size large enough to cover the earth's surface and we saw for the first time who we are as a people of God. Would we be able to comprehend the vast mystery of the earth's beauty and its billions of people living and dying every day? I think not.

Destiny is a peculiar thing and not one of us is stranger to it. For a period of time, we put socks on and come into this world in much the same way as our ancestors did and when we depart it's not the wardrobe that we take with us.

In our brief sojourn here, you might say – we're like trees growing. One day we're flourishing, green, tall and lovely. People see our beauty and then Someone picks the leaves off our branches. Wind comes and we sail home through the skies.

If the face of Love comes knocking at our door in this way, perhaps we will no longer fear death. Instead, we will begin to see it as a transfer of Energy where the purity of God filters the dust out of us no matter what wrongdoing we have done.

ABOUT THE AUTHOR

For the last 16 years, Eileen Curteis, a Sister of Saint Ann, has been involved in the Reiki Healing Ministry at Queenswood, a retreat and spirituality centre in Victoria, British Columbia. A former teacher, principal and educator for 27 years, Eileen shares that her greatest passion has always been in the literary arts. She is a poet, artist, writer and more recently a filmmaker, who has authored nine books to date.

Photograph by Stefan Jonsson

Eileen's literary works can be viewed on:
www.BooksOfExcellence.com

And her books can be purchased through Queenswood: www.QueenswoodVictoria.ca

www.ingramcontent.com/pod-product-compliance
Lightning Source LLC
Chambersburg PA
CBHW040936110426
42739CB00026B/10